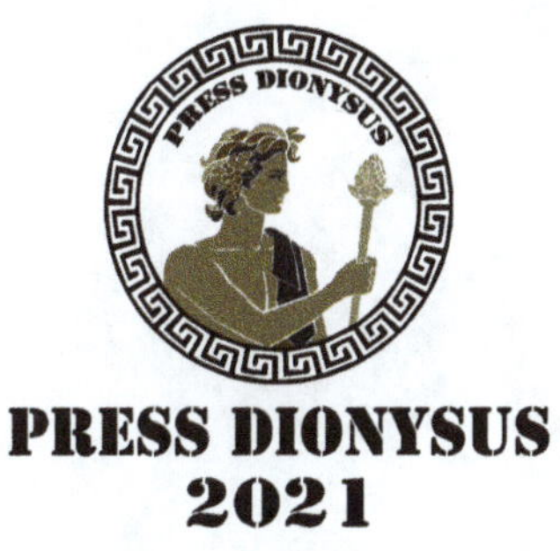

PRESS DIONYSUS
2021

First published in 2021 by PRESS DIONYSUS LTD in the UK, 167, Portland Road, N15 4SZ, London.

www.pressdionysus.com

ISBN: 978-1-913961-05-3

New Zealand

TRAVELERS STORY BOOK SERIES

Ozlem ISIK

Press Dionysus •
ISBN- 978-1-913961-05-3

© 2021 Press Dionysus
First Edition, July 2021, London

Book Design: S. Deniz Akıncı

Press Dionysus LTD, 167, Portland Road, N15 4SZ, London

• e-mail: info@pressdionysus.com
• web: www.pressdionysus.com

ABOUT THE AUTHOR:

The author has worked as an ESOL teacher and an interpreter in different countries. She has both B.A and M.A degrees in teaching a foreign language. She has developed a new, award winning method in teaching a foreign language. Anyone can learn both English and Turkish within 3 months using this new method and it is worldwide known. She lives in London, UK and continues to write story books and academic books on how to teach a foreign language.

ABOUT THE BOOK:

The book is designed and prepared for ESOL learners over 18 years of age. In the series which is called Travelers, there are different story books. The learner will comprehend, revise some basic English tenses, structures, phrases and have fun learning amazing facts about various countries in the world.

All learners will travel around the world and learn English at the same time.

This is a first in English teaching; improve your English skills and cultural knowledge.

Don't be sorry!

Read a story...

TRAVELERS STORY
BOOK SERIES
New Zealand

In this chapter, our heroes,
Carlo and Marcos are in
New Zealand
"The Land of Long White Cloud" now.
Australia
MADE IN ITALY
I ♥ NY
WELCOME TO THAILAND
The country looks like a long, white cloud.
LONG, WHITE CLOUD

The country has a lot of long, white clouds, long, white beaches and long, white mountains.

There are only around 4.8 million people in NZ and there are no snakes in the country.

The first European to arrive in New Zealand is the Dutch explorer Abel Tasman in 1642. It is also the first country to give women the right to vote in 1893.

Tasman sea
Auckland
Hobbiton
Maori Rock
Tongario National Park
Mountain Cook
Wellington
Christchurch
Moeraki Boulders Beach
Pacific ocean
NO SNAKES IN NEW ZEALAND

SEASONS IN DIFFERENT HEMISPHERES

Northern Hemisphere

SEASONS

WINTER	SPRING	SUMMER	AUTUMN

December	March	June	September
January	April	July	October
February	May	August	November

MONTHS

Southern Hemisphere

SEASONS

SUMMER	AUTUMN	WINTER	SPRING

December	March	June	September
January	April	July	October
February	May	August	November

MONTHS

As you know, their Italy tour was great.

Italy is a beautiful country with amazing food and friendly people. In Italy, they visited Rome (the capital), Milan, Venice and learned some Italian. (Ciao: hello, Ti amo: I love you). Italian is the language of love.

Our friends Carlo and Marcos are in Wellington now, the capital of New Zealand.

Wellington, the windy capital of New Zealand, is an amazing city, too. They are very excited to see it.

After a very long flight to New Zealand, they are tired and starving.

They want to taste the famous, national dessert Pavlova.

It is named after the Russian ballerina Anna Pavlova. Her tutu was the inspiration for the dessert.

Anna Pavlova

Pavlova Dessert

There are many pretty cafés around the city. The boys prefer a small, cosy one with pink, polka dotted curtains and a welcoming atmosphere. When you go in the café, a charming, sweet smell of cakes, desserts invade your nostrils first then your taste buds start to dance with delight and make you hungrier. First, they order some fizzy drinks with nice, small umbrellas in.

Then the infamous, mouth-watering Pavlova finally arrives at the table, it is a jaw dropping experience for them. It looks like a pure white wedding dress with an amazing crown decorated with many strawberries. It is crusty outside and soft inside with tasty notes and gentle touches of strawberry flavour. After eating the dessert, Marco says "Carlos, I think, I will order another Pavlova. You know I have a sweet tooth". They both laugh and sip their umbrella cocktails. "Life is good with good friends and great food and beverages" says Carlos.

LORD OF THE RINGS TRILOGY

THE MOVIE: LORD OF THE RINGS

The café is full of tourists from every corner of the world and an old, wooden bookcase seems a bit flirty and inviting with the world famous Trilogy (The Lord of The Rings) on one of its shelves. It was filmed in New Zealand by Sir Peter Jackson. When you watch the movie, you admire the breath-taking nature of New Zealand.

After enjoying their drinks and dessert, Marcos and Carlo are exhausted and want to go to their hotel to rest.

Their hotel is not so far away from the café so they decide to walk to the hotel. In New Zealand, you don't worry about street crime because it is a very safe country.

    In their hotel room they find a travel book and plan
their next day. The main museum in Wellington is "Te
Papa". They will go to the museum after breakfast the
next day.

They are so surprised to learn that New Zealanders are called Kiwis. Actually, kiwis are wingless birds. They cannot fly. Of course there is a fruit named kiwi as well. The kiwi fruit is actually from China. The fruit was named after kiwi bird because the brown skin of the kiwi fruit is similar to the feathers of the kiwi bird.

When they read the travel book, they start to learn more about New Zealand. The official languages in NZ are Maori and New Zealand Sign Language. English is the main national language. Some English words are really interesting and different. Here are some examples; (togs: swimsuit, jandals: flip flops, buggered: really tired).

In New Zealand if someone says "yeah-nah", it is a very casual way of saying "No, thank you".

They also learn that in NZ the sheep outnumber people. New Zealand has five sheep for every person.

New Zealand is an expensive country and the taxes are really high. New Zealand's currency is the New Zealand dollar. Before 1967, the currency was the New Zealand pound. It is also a nuke-free country. They don't want any nuclear power plants and nuclear weapons in the country.

The most popular career in the country is police officer.

Wellington is the windiest city in the world.

The Maori people are the first settlers of the country. They first arrived in NZ in 1200s from Polynesia. They have a unique culture. "Ta Moko" is the traditional art of tattooing in Maori culture.

Carlo and Marcos enjoy every line of the travel book very much and they decide to visit the other big cities in NZ. The other well-known big cities in NZ are Christchurch, Auckland and Hamilton.

After learning very interesting, fun facts about the country, they go to bed late but they are sure they will get up very early because they want to enjoy every second of the city tour. They know that the world is a book but if you do not travel, you can read only one page.

They look forward to meeting you again in another country soon.

EXERCISES

ANSWER THE FOLLOWING QUESTIONS

What is the capital city of NZ?

Can you give the names of two big cities in NZ?

What is the nickname of New Zealanders?

What is the currency in NZ?

What is "nuke-free"?

What is Pavlova?

Do you like travelling? Why (not)? Which countries do you want to see? Why?

"Travel opens the mind and hearts and make people better" What does the statement mean? Do you agree? Why (not)?

The Maoris arrived in NZ from .... over 1000 years before the Europeans. They are the first .... In NZ.

.... fruit is a healthy snack and is also a .... for New Zealanders.

In NZ the sheep .... people by 5 to 1.

.... is a series of three complete books, films or creative works.

.... is a criminal activity that happens in a public place.

After a very long day, they were .... and went straight to bed.

The weather was so .... that my umbrella turned inside out.

.... is a short skirt worn by ballerinas and dancers.

LIST:

exhausted, trilogy, tutu, kiwi, outnumber, windy, Polynesia, settlers, nickname, street crime

C   GROUP WORK (MAKING A POSTER)

Make a poster about a city or country you would like to visit and give some interesting / weird facts about it.

D   DISCUSSION

"Travelling- it first leaves you speechless then turns you into a story teller." What does this saying mean? Discuss it. Why do people travel? Is travelling important? Why (not)?

Write a short paragraph about the capital city of your own country.

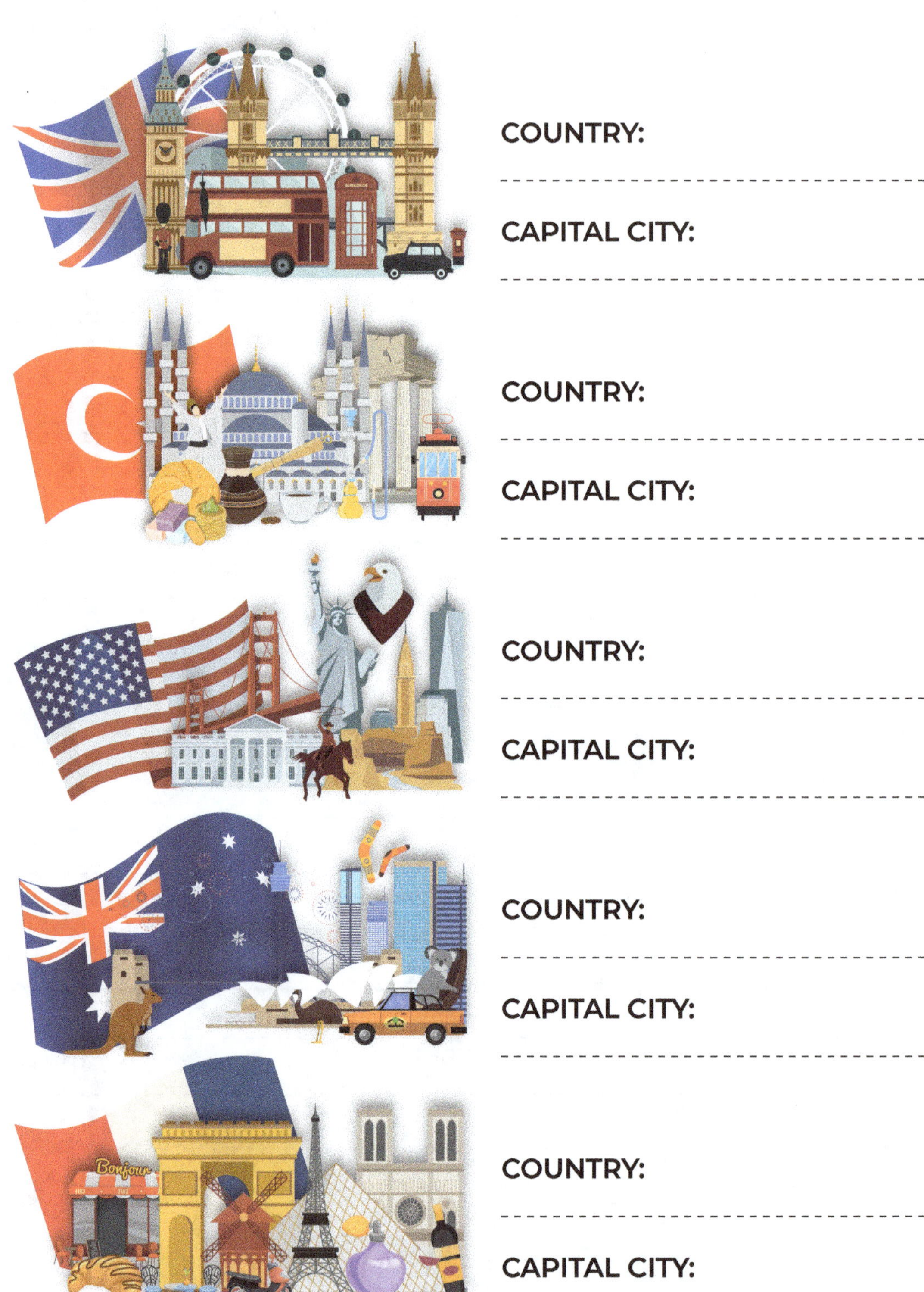

COUNTRY:

CAPITAL CITY:

COUNTRY:

CAPITAL CITY:

COUNTRY:

CAPITAL CITY:

COUNTRY:

CAPITAL CITY:

COUNTRY:

CAPITAL CITY:

ASK QUESTIONS TO THE UNDERLINED PARTS

The main museum in Wellington is Te Papa.

---?

No one worries about street crime in NZ because it is a very safe country.

---?

Kiwi birds are wingless. They cannot fly.

---?

The boys went to NZ by plane.

---?

Their school will start in September.

---?

MAKE A LIST OF THE FACTS YOU REMEMBER ABOUT NZ.

The capital city: ....

The warmest months in New Zealand: ....

The currency: ....

The windiest city: ....

Trilogy filmed in New Zealand: ....

The name of the traditional art of tattooing: ....

The famous, national dessert: ....

WORDS:

TUTU, PAVLOVA, TOGS, JANDALS, STARVING, KIWI, FIZZY DRINK, POLKA DOTTED CURTAINS, TE PAPA, MUSEUM, MAORI PEOPLE, WINDY, MAORI TATTOO

J MATCH THE WORDS WITH THE PICTURES

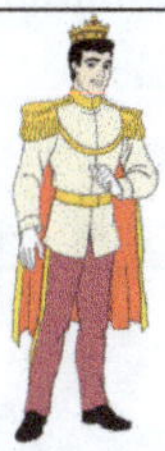	CUTE, LOVELY, CHARISMATIC	....
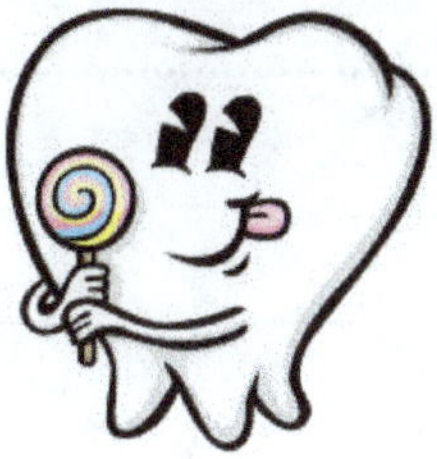	A GREAT LIKING FOR SWEET FOODS	....
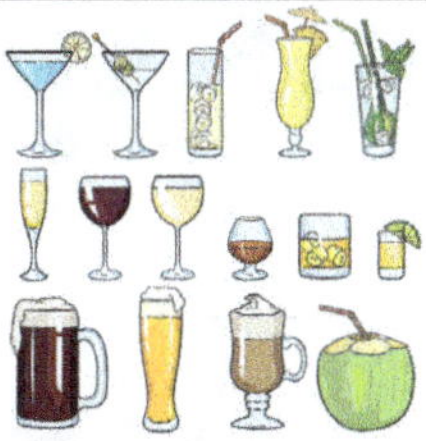	A DRINK BUT NOT WATER	....
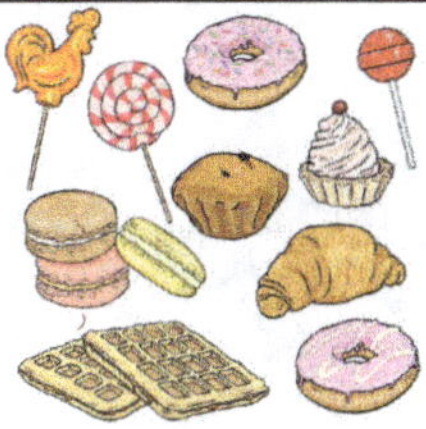	SWEET DISH	....
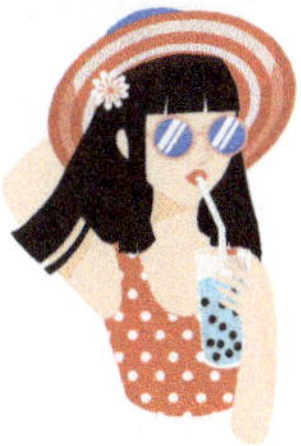	DRINK, TASTE	....
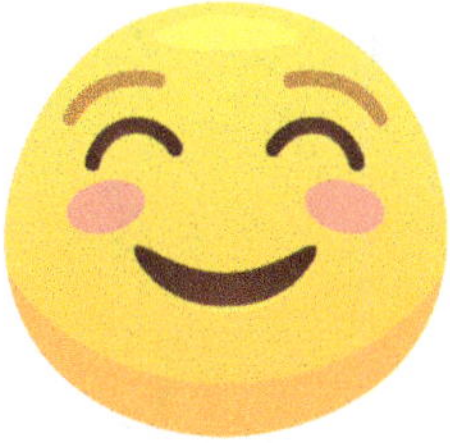	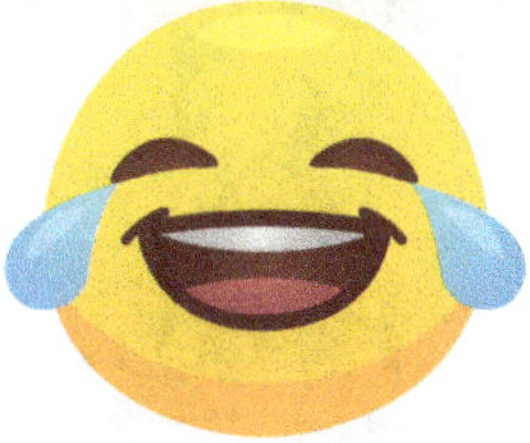	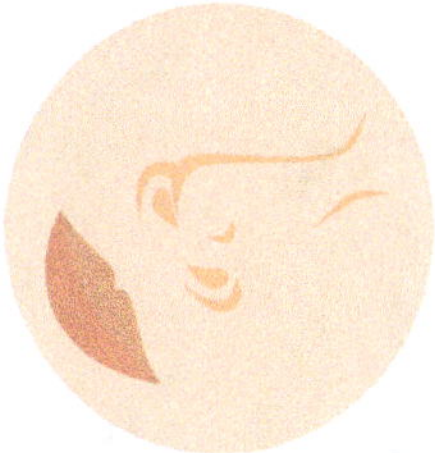 ....

	LITTLE POINTS ON THE SURFACE OF YOUR TONGUE. THEY ALLOW YOU TO RECOGNIZE THE FLAVOUR OF A FOOD/DRINK	....
	SMELLING, LOOKING DELICIOUS	....
	SURPRISING, SHOCKING	....

WORDS:

JAW DROPPING, BEVERAGE, CHARMING, SWEET TOOTH, DESSERT, SIP, SMILE, NOSTRILS, TASTE BUDS, LAUGH, MOUTH WATERING